World Rivers

Reader

Core Knowledge®

ISBN: 978-1-68380-040-8

World Rivers

Table of Contents

World Rivers
Reader
Core Knowledge History and Geography™

Chapter 1
Rivers Bring Life to Farms and Cities

The Nile River "Hey, over here!" A young boy waves to you with a smile. He invites you to join him on his small sailboat. "I can show you the Nile River!"

"Why should I see the Nile River?" you ask.

The boy can hardly believe anyone would ask such a question. "The Nile is one of the great rivers of the world. In fact, it's the longest river in Africa. It's also *the* longest river in the world, *and* the most important river in my country, Egypt!"

You look out across the Nile. There are boats of all kinds, large and small. The hot sun shines on the water. A breeze would feel good. So would a rain shower. Maybe it will be cooler out on the water.

The Nile River flows through the heart of Cairo, Egypt's capital.

"OK, let's go!" you say. Your new friend tells you his name is Ahmed (/ah*med/). He is in his early teens, and he earns money guiding tourists on the Nile River. Together, the two of you set off in Ahmed's boat. After a few minutes, you look back at the land. You see trees lined up on the **riverbank**. Behind the trees there is sand. It stretches as far as you can see into the distance. The Nile River flows right through the Sahara, the largest and one of the driest deserts in the world.

Cool Facts About the Nile River

- The Nile River looks black when it floods because of the color of the sediment it carries.

- Ancient Egyptians called the river Ar or Aur, which means "black."

"Nearly everyone in my country lives close to the Nile River," Ahmed says. "It's our main **source** of drinking water. It also provides the water that farmers use to grow food."

The Nile River is a wide and powerful river. It carries Ahmed's boat as if it were a feather. Suddenly you see something familiar in the distance.

"Do you see the Great Pyramids (/pihr*uh*mihdz/)?" Ahmed says, pointing to them proudly.

You remember learning about the pyramids in first grade. Now you decide to show off what you learned.

"Thousands of people worked for many years to build those pyramids," you say. "They brought huge blocks of stone to build them. They used boats on this river to carry the stone."

Ahmed nods in agreement.

It's hot, and you're getting thirsty. You think about all those workers sweating in the fierce sun to build the pyramids. "What did workers eat and drink out here in the desert?" you ask Ahmed.

"I think they drank water from the Nile," Ahmed replied. "Even though most of my country is desert, farmers have always grown plenty of food," he explains. "After all, they had to feed thousands of people living in cities. But the only way they could do it in this dry place was to use water from the Nile River for **irrigation** (/ihr*uh*gae*shun/).

"For thousands of years, we have depended on the river for irrigation of the farmers' crops. We say the river's water gives life to the farmers' thirsty crops."

The sun is setting in a golden sky. You and Ahmed make plans to visit the pyramids on another day.

The Nile River provides valuable water used to irrigate farmers' crops in the dry desert.

Huang He: The Yellow River

Another river that brings water to farmers' fields is what the Chinese call Huang He (/hwang/hee/)—the Yellow River. This river is in China on the continent of Asia, and its name comes from the yellow color of its water. That color comes from the tons of **silt** in the river.

> **Vocabulary**
> ....
> **silt,** n. tiny pieces of soil or earth carried by the water in a river
>
> **flow,** v. to move; water moves (or flows) downstream in a river

Now imagine you are traveling on this river. You see a young girl helping her father in a rice field near the Yellow River. You stop to ask the girl what she is doing.

"Why are you standing in this ditch?" you ask.

"I'm clearing out the weeds and twigs so the water can get through," she answers.

"Why do you have to do this?" you ask.

"We clean out the ditches used for irrigation so the water from the Yellow River can **flow** through them. The water brings life to our rice field," she answers.

"If we don't put water on our rice plants in exactly the right way," she continues, "the rice won't grow. If the rice doesn't grow, my family won't have rice to sell. We will lose money. Then I may not be able to get a new bicycle. That's what I'm saving my money for."

You smile at the girl. As you set off again down the river, you offer words of encouragement.

"I hope the rice grows and you get that bicycle!"

The Huang He, or Yellow River, gets its name from the color of its waters.

Chapter 2
Rivers Make Our Lives Better

Chang Jiang—The Yangtze River Whoosh! Your small boat is almost flying through crashing waters. You are on the Chang Jiang (/chang/jyang/), or Yangtze (/yang*see/) River, in China. The person in charge of your boat gives up trying to steer because the water is too wild.

The Big Question

Why do so many people settle close to major rivers?

"Oh no!" you shout. "Rocks ahead!" Everyone in the boat works hard to keep the boat from tipping over. Then your little boat shoots out like a cannonball fired from a cannon. Suddenly the boat slows down. The river becomes calm and peaceful.

You have just gone through one of the famous gorges of the Yangtze River, located on the continent of Asia. A gorge is a narrow space between two cliffs or mountains.

The Yangtze River travels through many different types of terrain, including mountains and gorges.

The Yangtze River is a mighty river. Like the Nile, it has supplied people with water for thousands of years. But in history, the Yangtze River has often caused **floods**. Time and again, the raging river has overflowed its banks. Floods have carried away crops, animals, and even people. A history of floods is one reason why China built a great **dam** on the river.

Have you ever read about the Great Wall of China? Well, the dam on the Yangtze River is sort of like the Great Wall built in water. It's as wide as twenty-two football fields. In fact, it's the largest dam in the world! It is called the Three Gorges Dam.

This huge dam holds back the mighty Yangtze River.

How do dams work? They slow and control a river's flow. The dam blocks much of a river's flowing water. It holds that water in large **reservoirs** (/reh*zuh*vwarz/). The reservoir behind the Three Gorges Dam is four hundred miles long. Dam operators let a little of this water flow out of the reservoir slowly and steadily. As a result, there are fewer floods.

Reservoirs also store water for drinking and for irrigating crops. In addition, dams use the power of flowing water to make electricity. This source of power helps many people and businesses in China.

The Indus River

Did you know that the Indus River is one of the longest rivers in Asia? The river's **sources** are in Tibet and India, and it flows through Pakistan to its **delta**. In ancient times, people living along the Indus River did not have computers or electricity. But they did build a great **civilization**. The river helped them do this.

Some 4,500 years ago, people living near the Indus River in present-day Pakistan built the city of Mohenjo-daro (/moe*hen*joe/dahr*oe/). This well-planned city had many amazing buildings and spaces. One of the most interesting is called the Great Bath. It was a pool about half the size of a basketball court. It was made of brick. Water for the

Four thousand five hundred years ago, people living along the Indus River built the city of Mohenjo-daro, with its Great Bath.

pool came from a well fed by the Indus River. The pool may have been used for some kind of religious ceremony.

The Ganges River

To many people in India, which is located in Asia, the water of the Ganges (/gan*jeez/) River is special. To followers of the Hindu religion, the Ganges is a holy river. Poets have written poems and songs about it. Sculptors have carved fountains and statues to honor it.

Many Indians call the Ganges River *Mother Ganges*. They use this name because the river brings life to dry lands. Each year, the dry season comes. It turns everything to dust. The Ganges River, however, still has water in it.

The river also brings life to the people in the country of Bangladesh (/bang*la*desh/). This is where the Ganges River's **mouth** is found. As the great river approaches its end near the Indian Ocean, it breaks into many small waterways. The water slows, and it drops the silt it has been carrying. The silt piles up at the mouth of the Ganges and forms a wedge of land called a delta.

Hindu pilgrims bathe in the Ganges River because they believe the water is holy.

Chapter 3
A River Viewed from Above

The Murray River The Murray River is the longest river in Australia. It is also a popular one for vacations. To really see this river, you need to be high up in the sky!

The Big Question

What is the difference between the source and the mouth of a river?

"Where do you want to start exploring the Murray River?" your pilot asks.

"Start at the beginning, please," you answer. "Let's go to the source of the river." The source is the very beginning of a river. Often, a river's source is a tiny trickle of water hidden away in hills or mountains.

Mount Kosciuszko is the tallest mountain in Australia and part of the Great Dividing Range.

The pilot turns the plane toward the southeastern corner of Australia. The plane lands on an unpaved strip of grass. You are now in the Great Dividing Range. These are Australia's highest mountains. The source of the Murray River is near Australia's highest peak, Mount Kosciuszko (/kah*zee*us*koe/). In the spring, melting snow flows down the hillsides and adds water to the streams below. You take a good look at the mountains before boarding the small plane again.

"Watch carefully below," the pilot says. "Soon the river will really look like a river."

The plane winds along between mountains. Soon you see a dark line on the ground below. The trickle of water at the river's source has become a river. After a while, another large river seems to flow into the Murray River. This is the Darling River. These two rivers drain the whole southeastern part of Australia. Experts use the term **drainage basin** to describe the whole area drained by a main river and other connected rivers.

Cool Fact About the Murray River
Parts of the Murray River in Australia have dried up at least three times.

"Make sure your seat belt is fastened," the pilot says. "We're going to land and take a closer look at the Murray River."

Now you are on the ground, alongside the river. The air is warm and dry. You see fields full of melons. There are **orchards** full of

16

An aerial view of the Murray River shows how it weaves through farmland and pastures.

vineyard, n. an area where grapes are grown on plants called vines

pasture, n. land set aside for cows, horses, or other animals to feed off the natural grasses

orange trees and **vineyards** with grapes growing on the vines. The fruits look juicy and sweet.

"Water from the Murray River is used by farmers for irrigation," the pilot tells you. "The hot summers are good for growing crops, but the crops need plenty of water in the heat."

So do you. The juice and water the pilot brought along are refreshing. As you drink, you admire the sheep and cattle eating the green grass in the **pasture**.

The River's Mouth

"Let's go to the mouth of the river now," the pilot says. "That's where the river ends and its waters empty into the ocean."

As you follow the river's path, you see what appear to be lakes below. Some are small, but some are quite large. In fact, these bodies of water are man-made lakes or reservoirs. They are made by dams that hold back or block the Murray River. The dams cause the river to back up and flood a large area to create reservoirs. From the plane, you can see sailboats, houseboats, and canoes on them.

"I like to come here with my wife and daughters on vacation," the pilot says. "We rent a houseboat to live on for a week or two. We

Dams along the Murray River create reservoirs.

like to swim and fish. Sometimes we go to one of the nature parks where we can see pelicans, kangaroos, and parrots."

"Sounds cool!" you say. The pilot turns the plane toward home. You sit back and relax as you fly high up in a beautiful clear sky.

Chapter 4
Dangers and Navigation Along Rivers

The Mississippi River In the 1850s, a young man named Sam was learning to be a **river pilot** on the mighty Mississippi River, located in North America.

The Big Question

What are the dangers boats face on rivers?

Vocabulary

"river pilot," (phrase), a person whose job is to guide boats safely on a river

A river pilot steers boats around dangerous places in a river. He brings people and cargo safely to shore. If he makes a mistake, all may be lost. It is a big responsibility. As Sam once said, "Your true [river] pilot cares nothing about anything on earth but the river, and his pride in his [job is greater than] the pride of kings."

The mighty Mississippi River contains many hazards.

Like many rivers, the Mississippi changes hour by hour. A stretch that was safe a week ago may be dangerous today. **Sandbars** form and shift. The water changes course. **Currents** roll logs over and hide them under the surface. River pilots have to watch out for signs of trouble. Tiny ripples or a dark patch in the water might hide a log or rock. These things can cause a wreck. There is a lot for river pilots to look out for!

Cool Fact About the Mississippi River

In 1927, the Mississippi River flooded. This historic flood moved enough water to fill twenty-six Olympic-size swimming pools every second.

The Mississippi has other rivers flowing into it. A river that flows into a larger river is called a **tributary** (/trih*byue*tehr*ee/). Two major tributaries of the Mississippi River are the Ohio River and the Missouri River. At places where rivers join, waters can be very tricky, and river pilots must be very careful.

Sam was helping out on a riverboat that carried a number of river pilots as passengers. They were checking on the logs, sandbars, and other dangers of the river. The pilots told each other about

In the 1800s, riverboats were a common sight on the Mississippi River.

their own travels. They asked each other questions. Sam learned a lot. But as the other pilots talked, Sam became more and more worried. Years later he remembered how he had felt.

Sam's full name was Samuel Langhorne Clemens. He wrote many stories about his days on the river. When he wrote these stories, he used the name Mark Twain.

Two of Mark Twain's best-known books are *The Adventures of Tom Sawyer* and *The Adventures of Huckleberry Finn*. These books are both set on the Mississippi River. They tell of the river's charm— and dangers. They are still popular today.

Tom, Joe and Huck on the raft

This scene from *The Adventures of Tom Sawyer* shows the characters Tom, Joe, and Huck on the Mississippi River.

The Ob River

You know that captains and pilots of boats face many dangers. In some places the dangers include ice.

One example is the Ob (/ahb/) River in Asia. This river's source is in the mountains of central Asia near Mongolia.

The Ob River flows north for hundreds of miles. It passes through **swamps**, forests, and vast **wastelands** of Siberia. Finally, the Ob reaches its mouth at the Arctic Ocean.

As the river flows north, the climate changes. Temperatures begin to drop below freezing. Ice forms on the river.

This ice creates the greatest danger along the Ob River. Boats that hit a large piece of ice can suffer serious damage. Winter begins early and lingers late in the Arctic. This means river pilots on the Ob must keep a close eye on the calendar and on the **thermometer**. If they launch their boats too early in the spring or too late in the fall, they may find huge ice blocks jamming northern stretches of the river. Because of the cold, ships can travel parts of this river for only a few months out of the year.

Vocabulary

swamp, n. a flat wooded area that is often flooded

wasteland, n. land that is not useful to people

thermometer, n. an object that measures the temperature of certain things, such as air or water

Chapter 5
Wildlife on Wild Rivers

The Amazon River Your canoe slips silently through the darkness. Strange sounds come from all around. Something gently brushes your arm. You hope it is a leaf!

The Big Question

How do rivers support wildlife?

You are in Brazil in South America. You are paddling down a tributary of the Amazon River. Your guide wants you to hear the rainforest sounds at night.

You were nervous before starting the canoe trip. Other tourists had gone swimming in the river during the day. They had joked about piranhas in the water. One man had said that a school of these small, fierce fish working together could eat a human being in a couple of minutes. This talk had made you nervous, and so you had chosen to stay on the riverbank.

Now, however, you are glad you are in a canoe. As you glide through the humid darkness, the guide asks you to look up into the thick trees. "You may not see much," she says. "But the monkeys, birds, and snakes can see you!"

Vocabulary

piranha, n. type of flesh-eating fish of South America that lives in fresh water

humid, adj. having a lot of moisture in the air

Riverbanks of the Amazon River and its tributaries support very dense vegetation.

You know that although the Amazon is the second longest river in the world, it carries more water than any other river. You also know that the lands along the Amazon support an amazing number of animals, reptiles, and insects. The Amazon is their home. They live here year-round.

This is a Brazilian Rainbow Boa.

Cool Fact About the Amazon River

The Amazon River has the world's largest drainage basin, and the Amazon carries more water than any other river in the world.

The next day, you paddle the final stretch of the tributary. Finally, you enter the Amazon River itself. You begin to see more canoes and fishing boats. But mostly you see rainforest. You also hear birds and insects chirping in the trees. In the daytime, it is sunny and hot on the river. When you tie up the canoe to explore, you find the forest refreshingly cool and shady.

Dozens of rivers flow into the Amazon. You have learned that the area into which a river's tributaries drain is called a *drainage basin*. The Amazon River has the world's largest drainage basin.

In places on your journey, you see what appear to be two rivers flowing side by side. This illusion is caused by the fact that some

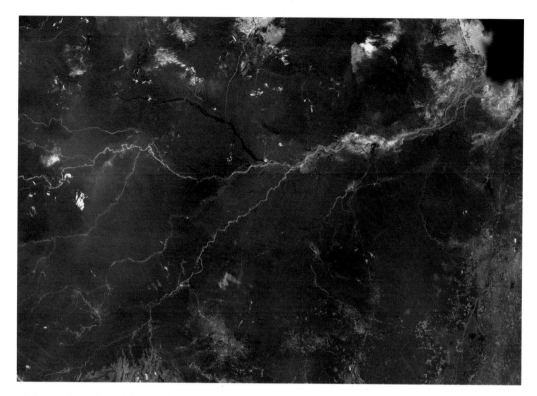

This satellite photo shows the Amazon River and some of the larger tributaries in the Amazon's drainage basin. There are many others that are too small to see.

tributaries are different in color. This difference is caused by many things including the presence of silt and decaying plants in the water. When a tributary of one color enters the waters of another color, it can take a while for the waters to mix.

The Orinoco River

After exploring the Amazon River, you set off to see the Orinoco (/or*uh*noe*koe/) River. This river shares much in common with the Amazon. It crosses the northern part of South America and empties into the Atlantic Ocean. Many boats travel up and down the river. You can find a boat tour with no problem.

As you travel along the Orinoco River, you see that the land to the north is wild and beautiful. Venezuelans (/ven*uh*zway*lunz/)

Water plunges over 3,200 feet down from Angel Falls in Venezuela.

call it the Llanos (/yah*noes/). Cattle ranchers share this land with monkeys, anteaters, crocodiles, and other wildlife.

The land to the south of the river is even wilder. Its mountains contain the world's highest **waterfall**, Angel Falls. You have heard that the sight of Angel Falls takes a person's breath away. You would love to see it.

Vocabulary

waterfall, n. a place where water flows over the edge of a cliff

Arctic Ocean, n. one of the four major oceans, located in the Northern Hemisphere. It is the smallest and shallowest of the world's major oceans

Northern Hemisphere, n. the half of the earth located north of the equator

migrate, v. to move to a different place

The Mackenzie River

You have enjoyed the warm weather of South America. But you know there are great rivers in colder areas. In school you learned that in Canada, a long river called the Mackenzie flows north from the Rocky Mountains. It stretches all the way to the **Arctic Ocean**, which is located in the **Northern Hemisphere**. On the way, it flows through many lakes and swampy areas. With its tributaries, it covers a huge drainage basin in northwestern Canada.

During the long Arctic winter, the river is frozen solid for months. But during Canada's short summer, the Mackenzie River comes alive.

Thousands of geese, ducks, swans and other birds spend the summer along the river. They feed on grasses and short plants that grow in the summer's warmth. When winter comes, the birds **migrate**. They fly south in search of warmer weather.

You wonder what it would be like to explore a river such as this!

Chapter 6
Three Rivers and Many Waterfalls

The Iguaçu River Imagine a waterfall so powerful that its water "boils with foam." The water "hurls itself into space." It then tumbles over a cliff and crashes below with enough force to shake the earth.

The Big Question
....

How do rapids and waterfalls affect river travel?

Such a waterfall really exists. It is called Iguaçu (/ee*gwuh*soo/) Falls, and it is one of the biggest waterfalls in the world. Iguaçu Falls creates huge clouds of mist that rise into the air. It looks like water is flowing up to the sky!

The Iguaçu Falls are almost three times wider than Niagara Falls.

Iguaçu Falls is located in southern Brazil on the Iguaçu River in South America. The Iguaçu River is a tributary of the Paraná River. Of course, boats cannot go over the falls. But at the river's mouth on the Atlantic Ocean, large ships can sail up the river. In fact, ships can travel a full four hundred miles up the Iguaçu. They can reach Paraguay (/par*uh*gway/). This river traffic is very important for Paraguay. You see, Paraguay is a **landlocked** country. It has no ocean coast. The river helps people in Paraguay get goods to and from other countries.

> **Vocabulary**
>
> **landlocked,** adj. cut off from the seacoast; surrounded by land
>
> **rapids,** n. place on a river where the water moves swiftly and violently

The Congo River

Now imagine a wide river in the middle of Africa. This river has many small waterfalls and islands in it. This is the Congo River. It rises from its source in central Africa. From there, it flows in a long curve to the Atlantic Ocean.

Cool Fact About the Congo River
Tigerfish in the Congo River often hunt in groups. They have very sharp teeth and sometimes eat large animals.

It is impossible for boats to travel too far on the Congo River. Sooner or later they have to stop because of **rapids**, islands,

Fish traps in the raging Congo River

and other dangers. Today there is a railroad along the part of the river where boats cannot pass. Boats pull over at one end of the railroad. Their passengers and cargo are moved onto trains. Then the trains carry everything to the other end of the railroad. Everything is loaded onto other boats to continue the journey.

The Yukon River

It is risky to ignore the danger of rivers! In 1897 thousands of people learned this the hard way on the Yukon River in Canada, located in North America.

At first, the people were excited! They had heard that people were finding gold in the Klondike. This is an area where the Yukon River and the Klondike River meet. People rushed to the Klondike. They hoped to find gold and get rich.

Few of these travelers knew much about the Klondike. They didn't know there were small waterfalls in the Yukon River. They probably would not have cared, anyway. Their minds were on one thing—gold! So, they hiked up mountain trails to a lake near the source of the Yukon River. There they quickly built simple boats to sail down the Yukon to the gold fields. They used anything they could get their hands on to build their boats.

At the end of May, some eight hundred boats headed down the river. About 150 of them were wrecked on the way. Ten people drowned. In their hurry, those seeking gold often put too many people on their boats.

Nearly one hundred thousand people tried to follow the Yukon River to the gold fields. Historians tell us that while many did find some gold, not quite so many "struck it rich!"

The Klondike River joins the Yukon River in what is today Dawson City in Canada.

Chapter 7
Rivers and Trade

The Rhine River Did you know that there really are castles like the ones in fairy tales? Many old castles stand along the rivers of Europe.

The Big Question
....

Why are the Rhine, Danube, Volga, and Niger rivers so important to the countries they flow through?

The Rhine River has many castles along its banks. People built them for protection against enemy attacks. A castle often has tall towers with windows at the top. From there, a lookout could see an enemy coming from far away.

The Rhine River flows past many castles.

Vocabulary

toll, n. money charged for use of a road or waterway

Castles also have thick stone walls. These made it hard for an enemy to break through. Still, castles along the Rhine were destroyed and rebuilt many times.

Building and owning a castle was not cheap! Castle owners stopped boats on the river. They made boats pay a **toll** to pass safely. The Rhine always had lots of traffic. Castle owners collected a lot of money.

The Rhine is still busy today. In fact, it is one of the world's busiest rivers. This is especially true near the Rhine's mouth at the North Sea. Many cargo ships and passenger boats sail these waters. Captains must be very careful.

The Danube River

You can also find castles along the Danube River. Both the Rhine and the Danube have their sources in Central Europe. The Rhine flows mainly toward the north. The Danube flows to the east. It glides through valleys, forests, cities, and plains. Finally, it reaches its mouth at the Black Sea.

The Danube touches seven countries. The river is so important to these countries that their leaders long ago made a promise. They agreed that everyone could use the river, even when their countries disagree about other things.

Cool Fact About the Danube River

Ancient Greek sailors conducted trade along the Danube River, and ancient Romans patrolled its waters.

The Volga River

Far to the east of the Rhine and Danube rivers is Russia's most important river. It is called the Volga River. Russian folk songs call the Volga *Beloved Mother*. That's because so many people depend on it. Russians use the Volga to deliver food, coal, lumber, and **manufactured goods**.

The Volga flows into the Caspian Sea. It does not flow directly into an ocean. A **network** of rivers and **canals** links the

Cranes stand ready to load or unload cargo from ships on the Volga River.

Volga to the Baltic Sea and to the Black Sea. From the Baltic Sea, ships can reach the Atlantic Ocean. From the Black Sea, they can sail to the Mediterranean Sea. The Volga helps Russia stay connected by water with other countries.

The River Niger

Sometimes the cities on riverbanks reveal how important the river is. The city of Timbuktu in the African nation of Mali is one example. It is located along the Niger River.

Over five hundred years ago, Timbuktu was the capital of a mighty African empire. It was also a great trading center. Its bazaar (/buh*zahr/), or marketplace, was a busy place. The shouts of buyers and sellers filled the air. Smelly camels strolled the streets. Vendors sold salt, ivory, wooden statues, and copper rings. The air smelled of sweet watermelons and grilled fish and onions.

These and many other goods moved up and down the Niger River on boats. Traders passed hippopotamuses bathing lazily in the water. Nearby, fishing boats caught fish for market.

Even today, local marketplaces still depend on the Niger River. People in Western Africa still use the river to carry goods. The hustle and bustle of their marketplaces remind us that civilization not only springs up, but still prospers by the riverside.

Even today, camels are a common sight on the streets of Timbuktu.

Three Major Rivers of Africa

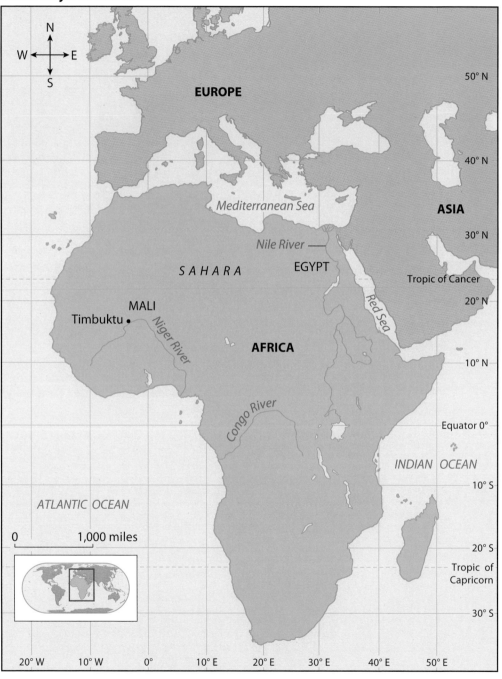

Atlas

Some Major Rivers of North America

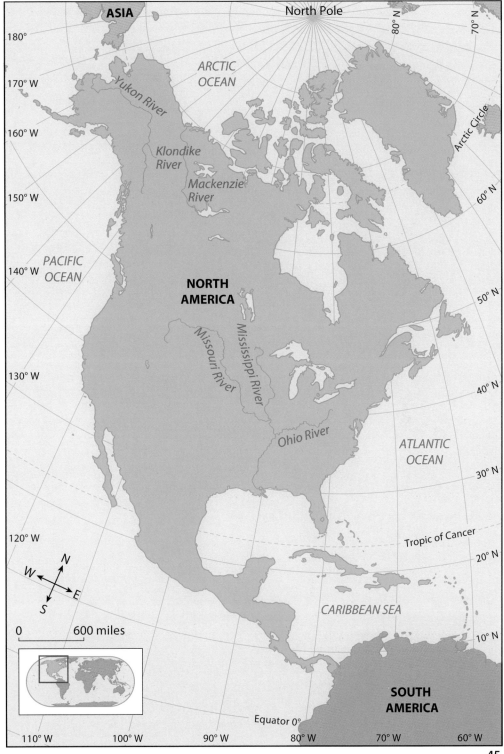

Atlas

Three Major Rivers of South America

Atlas

Three Major Rivers of Europe

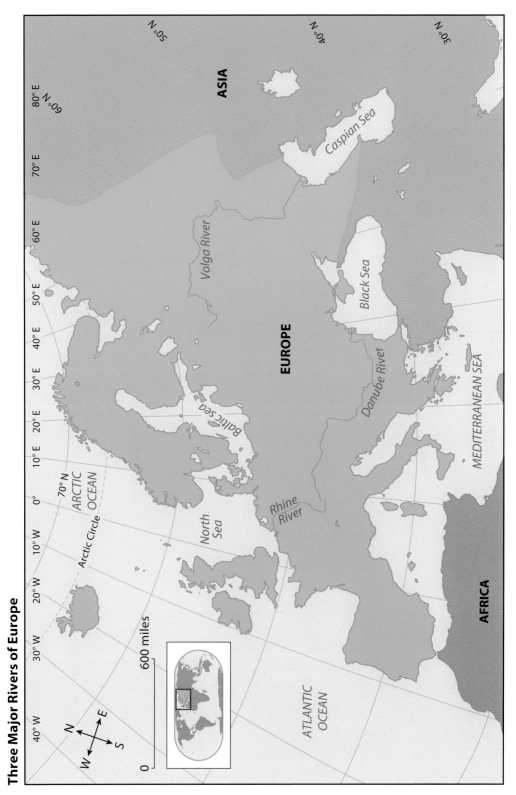

Atlas

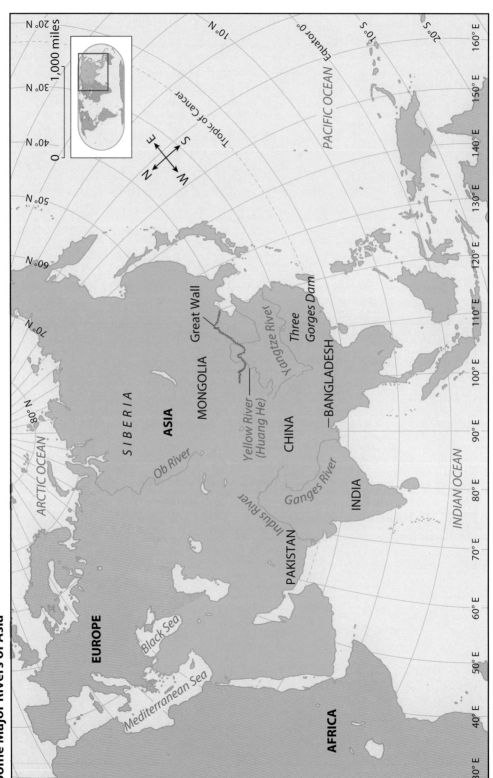

Some Major Rivers of Asia

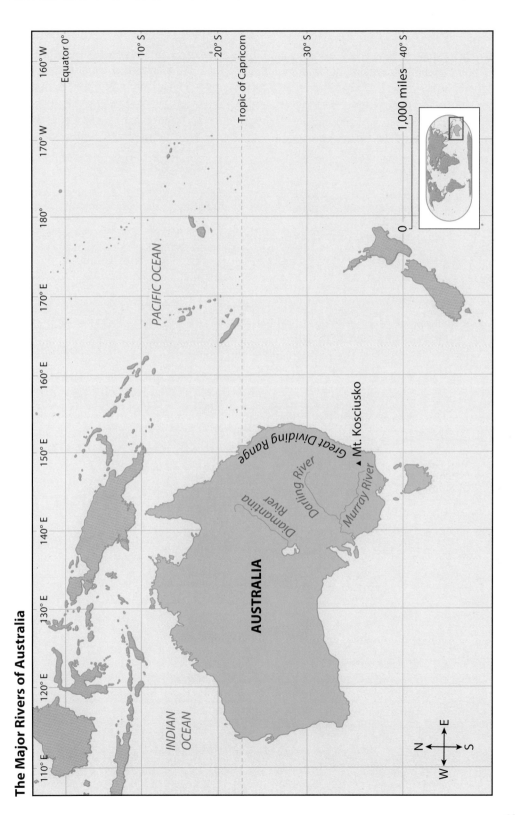

The Major Rivers of Australia

Glossary

A

Arctic Ocean, n. one of the four major oceans, located in the Northern Hemisphere. It is the smallest and shallowest of the world's major oceans **(31)**

C

canal, n. a channel dug by people, used by boats or for irrigation **(41)**

civilization, n. a society, or group of people, with similar religious beliefs, customs, language, and form of government **(11)**

current, n. the ongoing movement of water, such as in a river **(22)**

D

dam, n. a structure that blocks a flowing river and allows water to fill in behind it **(10)**

delta, n. land created by silt deposits at the mouth of a river **(11)**

drainage basin, n. the area drained by a main river and other connected rivers **(16)**

F

flood, n. what happens when a river overflows its banks **(10)**

flow, v. to move; water moves (or flows) downstream in a river **(6)**

H

humid, adj. having a lot of moisture in the air **(26)**

I

irrigation, n. watering of crops by moving water from a well, a river, or a lake, to a place where it does not rain enough to grow crops **(5)**

L

landlocked, adj. cut off from the seacoast; surrounded by land **(34)**

M

"manufactured good," (phrase), item made in large numbers for sale or trade **(41)**

migrate, v. to move to a different place **(31)**

mouth, n. the place where a river empties into a sea or other large body of water **(13)**

N

network, n. a connected system such as roads or waterways **(41)**

Northern Hemisphere, n. the half of the earth located north of the equator **(31)**

O

orchard, n. an area where a large number of fruit trees have been planted **(16)**

P

pasture, n. land set aside for cows, horses, or other animals to feed off the natural grasses **(18)**

piranha, n. type of flesh-eating fish of South America that lives in fresh water **(26)**

R

rapids, n. place on a river where the water moves swiftly and violently **(34)**

reservoir, n. a lake created by people for the purpose of storing water **(11)**

river, n. a body of moving or flowing water that follows a set path **(2)**

riverbank, n. the land at the edge of a river **(4)**

"river pilot," (phrase), a person whose job is to guide boats safely on a river **(20)**

S

sandbar, n. a buildup of sand formed by the movement of flowing water **(22)**

silt, n. tiny pieces of soil or earth carried by the water in a river **(6)**

source, n. a supply where an item such as water can be obtained **(4)**

source, n. the starting point or beginning of a river's water **(11)**

swamp, n. a flat wooded area that is often flooded **(25)**

T

thermometer, n. an object that measures the temperature of certain things, such as air or water **(25)**

toll, n. money charged for use of a road or waterway **(40)**

tributary, n. a stream or smaller river that flows into a larger river **(22)**

V

vineyard, n. an area where grapes are grown on plants called vines **(18)**

W

wasteland, n. land that is not useful to people **(25)**

waterfall, n. a place where water flows over the edge of a cliff **(31)**

Core Knowledge®

CKHG™
Core Knowledge HISTORY AND GEOGRAPHY™

Series Editor-In-Chief
E.D. Hirsch, Jr.

Editorial Directors
Linda Bevilacqua and Rosie McCormick

Subject Matter Expert

Charles F. Gritzner, PhD, Distinguished Professor Emeritus of Geography, South Dakota State University

Illustration and Photo Credits